P9-DDU-869

All Aboard!

All departing passengers for the land of *Hidden Ohio* should step up to platform 17!

Grab your backpacks and hop on to the Buckeye Express as we take you on a journey of fun discovery.

Make sure you get a window seat on this wild trip through different regions of the 17th State of the Union! Just as you would on a real train ride, make sure to keep your eyes open for many surprises along the way.

Full steam ahead as you look for all the fun hidden pictures on each page. Make sure to switch the book up side down, sideways and even in front of a mirror to track down all the concealed items!

The whistle is blowing, so that means it is time for this train to pull out of the station.

Before you go, make sure to check out the conductor and the various passengers on the front cover, and you'll discover many of our great Ohio state symbols! You should find the cardinal, the white trillium, the black racer snake, the Ohio State flag, scarlet carnation, ladybug, white-tailed deer, *Isotelus* and of course, a Buckeye!

Let's go ride the rails together!

Hidden
OHIO

Written by **Julie K. Rubini**
Rhymes by **Anne Margaret Lewis**
Illustrated by **Diana Magnuson**

Mackinac Island Press

for the love of reading

Holy Toledo!

Have you ever heard the phrase Holy Toledo? Toledo was given this nickname due to the many churches that line Collingwood Boulevard.

With glass blowing and kabooms,
there's plenty here to explore.
Tip toe around the zoo,
and hear the lions and tigers roar!

Do you want to see some animal antics? Then stop off at the Toledo Zoo for a fun day! Ride by train through the African Savanna, go underground with the polar bears, seals and hippos, hang tall with the giraffes, and hang loose with the monkeys and apes.

Calling all young paleontologists! Come dig for fossils at Fossil Park in Sylvania.

Search for...

 Owens bottle

 1929 Model A Ford Snooks Dream Cars

 Buckeye

 Hot dog

 Suckers

The world's first automated bottle blowing machine was created by inventor, Michael J. Owens, in 1903. With the help of Edmund Drummond Libbey, he started the Owens Bottle Company. They teamed up with the Illinois Glass Company, and now call themselves Owens-Illinois.

Have you ever seen a glass blower? You can, at the Toledo Museum of Art's Glass Pavilion in Toledo, where they honor their glass-making heritage. Toledo is known as the Glass Capital of the United States.

10 million Dum Dum Pops® a day are made at the Spangler Candy Company in Bryan. It's been around since 1906, and was founded by Arthur G. Spangler. In the summer you can visit and see how they make Dum Dum's, candy canes, and more.

Blue-Berry Jam

Come fly with thousands of butterflies at the Butterfly House in Whitehouse!

Kaboom! The reenactments at Fort Meigs complex in Perrysburg are filled with Kabooms. The reconstructed fort and museum sit on this original War of 1812 battle site.

Step back in time at Sauder Village and learn how the Black Swamp was settled in the 1800's. Step into a one room school house, watch a printer at work, and even learn to preserve jelly in the old farm house.

Can you find the Etch A Sketch on this page? It was originally invented in the late 1950's by a French electrician, Andre Cassagnes, and was made in Bryan, Ohio.

Vacationland

Opened in 1870 as a public bathing beach, Cedar Point is awesome! Switchback Railway was their first rollercoaster in 1892 and stood a mere 25 feet tall with a top speed of 10 mph. Compare that to the 2003 roller coaster, the Top Thrill Dragster at 420 feet tall and 120 mph, the second tallest and fastest roller coaster in the world.

More than 3 million people visit Cedar Point each year between May and October.

Discover Crystal Cave,
it's sure to make you grin.
Ride the Rippin' Raptor,
your head will surely spin.

The Lake Erie Islands Region is considered one of the "hottest" bird watching areas in North America! Grab your binoculars and spot one of over 300 species of birds on the 2000 acre wetland, Magee Marsh Wildlife Area.

How would you like to join a wildlife safari? Well you can, at the African Wildlife Safari Park in Port Clinton. You can feed the animals right from your car.

Search for...

Snoopy

Beach ball

Buckeye

Jet ski

Warbler

Ferry

Marblehead Lighthouse is the oldest lighthouse in continuous operation on the Great Lakes! The beacons have guided sailors along the Lake Erie shores of the Marblehead Peninsula since 1822.

Come visit the Perry's Victory and International Peace Memorial, standing 352 feet tall, and towering over South Bass Island and the town of Put-In-Bay. It honors those who fought in the Battle of Lake Erie, during the War of 1812.

On South Bass Island is Crystal Cave. It is claimed to be the world's largest geode— it's big enough to stand inside, and is 40 feet below ground level.

On Kelley's Island there is a 400 foot long by 35 foot wide gash of prehistoric grooves embedded into native limestone bedrock. These "glacier grooves" are the result of the Wisconsinan glacier, which retreated 12,000 years ago. You might also look for Inscription Rock to find pictographs of men, birds, and animals that were carved by the Erie Indians.

Cleveland Rocks!

*We're Rockin' and Rollin'
in a city full of jive,
exploring and creating
where science comes alive.*

Inventor Charles F. Brush installed
the first electric streetlights on
Cleveland's Public Square in 1879.
Growing up on Walnut Hills Farm
he first used a horse-drawn treadmill that would
power his dynamo to generate electricity with his
new machine. He later improved on the dynamo and
created a more efficient arc lamp that would be used
in these streetlights. Good job, Charles!

"The Man of Steel," otherwise known as
Superman, was created by Cleveland writer, Jerry
Siegel and artist, Joe Shuster, in 1938.

Sometimes out of bad, comes good. The
Cuyahoga River Fire of 1969, caused by pollution
in the waterway, helped lead the way to the
Clean Water Act of 1972.

Search for...

Baseball bat

Book

Buckeye

Magnifying glass

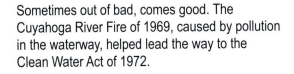
Guitar

Calling all sports fans! Come visit Cleveland, home to the Cleveland Cavaliers basketball team, the Cleveland Browns football team, and the Cleveland Indians baseball team. Go Cleveland!

Cleveland was named after Revolutionary War General Moses Cleaveland when he arrived in 1796 to plan out a city. Later in 1832, the first 'a' of Cleaveland was dropped when the masthead of the local paper, The Cleaveland Gazette and Commercial Register, was one letter too small to accommodate the full name, thus the city's current name, Cleveland.

Go wild at the Cleveland Metroparks Zoo, where you can see a Black Howler Monkey, a Masai Giraffe, a Persian Leopard, and much, much more!

On the shores of Lake Erie, in downtown Cleveland sits the cool glass pyramid that houses the Rock and Roll Hall of Fame. Cleveland disc jockey Alan Freed termed the phrase "rock and roll!" Bring your walking shoes because this Hall of Fame is 150,000 square feet of pure rock and roll.

Science comes alive at the Great Lakes Science Center with more than 400 hands-on exhibits. This super-sized six-story-high domed screen OMNIMAX® Theater hosts a projector weighing in at 4,200 lbs.

LakeShore and More!

From Lake Erie to Pymatuning,
let's have some outdoor fun!
Grab your skis and hike the trails
to see a White-tail on the run!

Dig your toes into the largest natural sand beach in Ohio at The Headlands State Park.

First established in 1869, Geneva-On-The-Lake was the first summer resort in Ohio. So bring your bathing suits and be ready for some camping and fishing, because your summer fun begins here.

Double trouble! On the first weekend of every August, Twinsburg hosts the annual Twins Day Festival where over 2000 sets of twins, both young and old, come together to celebrate.

Search for...

Sailboat

Waterskier

Buckeye

Picnic table

White-tailed deer

Are you plant crazy? Visit the Holden Arboretum near Kirtland. This is one of the country's largest arboreta with 19,230 plants from woody to wild!

Cross over the Alpine Valley covered bridge and you are in the snow belt of Ohio at the Alpine Valley Ski area. So if the slopes are your fancy, grab your boards, hop on, and enjoy the sprawling six slopes of pure snow fun! Yahoo!

Ashtabula County celebrates their covered bridges each year at the annual Covered Bridge Festival. In 2008 the county celebrated ONE BIG BRIDGE! A 600 foot timber covered bridge. This is the longest in our country, the 4th longest in the world, and will span the Ashtabula River." That's one long bridge!

Pymatuning (an Indian term for "crooked mouth man's dwelling place") State Park was created out of an area of swamp that the white man avoided settling. Dams were created in 1933, creating the reservoir in the park. The ducks and fish are the show in the Pymatuning Spillway!

Look up in the sky and you might see The Goodyear Blimp—not just one, but three. The blimps represent The Goodyear Tire and Rubber Company located in Akron. At the Goodyear World of Rubber Museum you can see a moon buggy, an artificial heart, and learn about how Charles Goodyear accidentally discovered the vulcanization process of rubber.

The Pro Football Hall of Fame is a must see. It officially opened its doors to the public in 1963, in Canton. The museum now has over 83,000 square-feet of museum space. So don't miss seeing all of the greats of football right here in Canton, Ohio.

It's a bird, it's a plane, it's a blimp,
and tires in the sky.
There's a mansion full of rooms
for you to play…'I spy.'

If your mouth isn't watering before you go in, it will by the time you come out of Harry London Candies. Tour the factory and watch how over 500 varieties of chocolates are made.

Search for...

| Carnation | Pennies | 2 Buckeyes | Flag | Football |

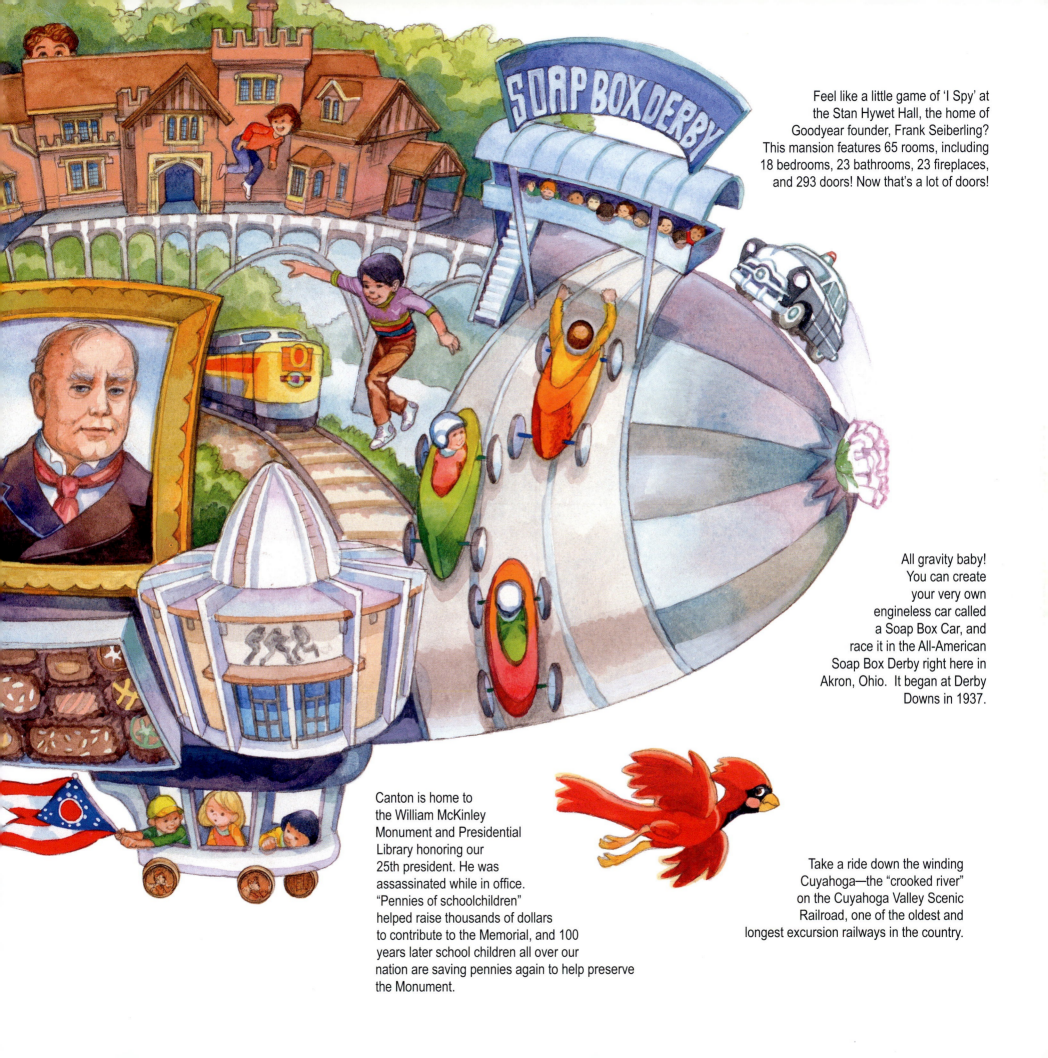

Feel like a little game of 'I Spy' at the Stan Hywet Hall, the home of Goodyear founder, Frank Seiberling? This mansion features 65 rooms, including 18 bedrooms, 23 bathrooms, 23 fireplaces, and 293 doors! Now that's a lot of doors!

SOAP BOX DERBY

All gravity baby! You can create your very own engineless car called a Soap Box Car, and race it in the All-American Soap Box Derby right here in Akron, Ohio. It began at Derby Downs in 1937.

Canton is home to the William McKinley Monument and Presidential Library honoring our 25th president. He was assassinated while in office. "Pennies of schoolchildren" helped raise thousands of dollars to contribute to the Memorial, and 100 years later school children all over our nation are saving pennies again to help preserve the Monument.

Take a ride down the winding Cuyahoga—the "crooked river" on the Cuyahoga Valley Scenic Railroad, one of the oldest and longest excursion railways in the country.

Take a minute to "smell the roses" in the rolling hills of Holmes County, Ohio where every state route is a scenic byway—beautiful and off the beaten path, with many Amish Farms.

We have spelling bees and the Amish have quilting bees, where the women come together as a community to make hand made quilts.

Horses, harvests, and sewing are part of Amish Land. The Amish live in peace where neighbors lend a hand.

LEHMAN'S

Holmes County and the surrounding counties have the largest population of Amish in the country. Upon their arrival in America in the 1700's they originally settled in Pennsylvania, then onto Ohio and Indiana.

Search for...

Corn

Cow

Buckeye

Pie

Amish crib

YODEL-LLAYAE

Come on over to a good old fashioned Barn Raising in Amish country where the framing of a barn is usually completed before the noon-day meal. This is a community event for the Amish, where entire families help to work on the barn. Don't forget your hammer and nails!

Buttons, buttons, buttons! Come visit the button house to see over 70,000 buttons on display at the Warther Museum in Dover.

Don't forget to visit Dreamsville USA in Dennison, Ohio. During WWII the troops were greeted with a smile and a free cup of coffee at the Dennison Railroad Depot.

Do you like cheese? Fruit? Vegetables? You will get plenty of all three in Amish Country. They are known for their wonderful harvests, handcrafted furnishings and homemade quilts.

The Warther Carving Museum in Dover features the life works and collections of Ernest and Frieda Warther. Ernest earned the title of "World's Master Carver" in the 1920's. His walnut wood, ebony, and ivory carved steam engine train replicas are amazing!

Come on over to the Sternwheeler Festival every weekend after Labor Day and you might see Betty Lou, a triple-decker, 100 foot long steel frame paddle boat, and 30 to 35 other sternwheeler and sidewheeler boats rollin' down the river. Splish, splash on the Ohio River!

Take a safari at the Wilds,
come home with many tales.
Paddle wheel down the river,
near miles of forest trails.

OHIO STERNWHEELER FESTIVAL

Ponds, ponds, and more ponds! At the Wayne National Forest there are over 500 acres of ponds to fish in, and over 300 miles of trails. There are over 833,990 acres in this forest. These lands help protect and preserve our country's forests.

Search for...

Binoculars

Hiking boot

Buckeye

U.S. Army button

Cheetah

Journey back in time at the Marietta Soda Fountain and Museum, featuring soda pop memorabilia, an old jukebox, and an old fashioned soda fountain! Swirl on the swivel stools at an old fashioned counter while you have a good ole fashioned lunch. Yum!

Named after Queen Marie Antoinette of France, Marietta has the proud distinction of being the first permanent, organized settlement in the Northwest Territory, established in 1788. Now that's a long time ago.

Fort Harmar, now Harmar Village was established in 1785. Visit historic Harmar Village where you can learn about a historic time over two centuries ago. Don't forget to stop off at the Ohio River Museum and the Toy and Doll Museum, too.

Rhinos, giraffes and bison, oh my! The Wilds, in Cumberland, has open range safaris on its 10,000 acres of prairie, woodlands, and wetlands. Come face to face with a cheetah or African wild dog in the Carnivore center. And don't forget to sign up for one of the great "WildeCamps" in the summer.

Sewah Studios, Inc. (est. 1927), of Marietta, OH, has installed approximately 1500 historical markers across Ohio. As you find them, you will discover the rich history that Ohio has to offer.

Cool Caves

Hockhocking or "Bottle River" is the name that the Wyandot, Delaware, and Shawnee Indian tribes gave to their river in the mid 1700's. It comes from the bottle-shaped valley of the Hocking River. The formation came to be from a glacial ice blockage many, many years before.

Glaciers have great effects on our world and they changed the climate of all Ohio to a moist, cool environment. This still remains in the deep gorges of Hocking County, and has created the towering eastern hemlocks, the Canada yew and the yellow and black birch. Nature is so powerful!

Explore in 'Old Man's Cave,' and chug on down the track. See the rushing waterfalls, while riding on horseback.

While you're at the Hocking Hills State Park make sure to visit the Cedar Falls. But don't get confused by the name, the Cedar Falls is actually surrounded by eastern hemlocks!

800 lunch boxes is a lot of lunches! That's what you'll see at Etta's Lunchbox café in the Hocking Hills area. Let's do LUNCH!

Search for...

Pick ax

Shovel

Buckeye

Camera

Lunch bucket

Caves and waterfalls
and deep, deep gorges
are exciting and fun in the
Hocking Hills State Park. Come
see the exposed bedrock that was
deposited over 350 million years ago.

The beautiful Hocking Valley area was once a huge coal
mining area. Almost 290 million years ago, rich deposits
of coal were laid down in this area and it has played a major
economic role in southeastern Ohio ever since. The history is rich.

The Ancient Adena Native culture existed in this area approximately 7,000
years ago, as proven by the ancient artifacts of their culture that have
been found. The Adena survived by hunting, fishing, and gathering wild
plants, and it was found that they lived in villages.

Est. 1804

From Nelsonville to Logan make sure to take a ride back in time on
the Hocking Valley Scenic Railway. Join their special Easter Bunny or
Santa rides. They're always a lot of fun!

In 2004 Ohio University of Athens celebrated its 200th
anniversary. Happy Anniversary Ohio University!

Thomas Worthington, one of Ohio's first U.S. Senators, its sixth governor, and known as "Father of Ohio Statehood," built a beautiful mansion in Chillicothe in 1807. Take a tour through the home and just imagine his family, including his wife and ten children living here!

Visit the original farm and restaurant just outside of Rio Grande to learn about Bob Evans, his early sausage making and hog raising days, and the original Bob Evans Restaurant that was opened in 1962. It was originally called "The Sausage Shop."

'Tecumseh!' is the outdoor drama and exciting display of flintlock firing and stage combat, and includes a 21 foot headfirst jump! This play shares the story of the great Shawnee Tribe leader's attempts to defend his sacred homelands in Ohio in the late 1700's. You can see it June through August at the Sugarloaf Mountain Amphitheatre near Chillicothe.

Welcome to Chillicothe
in the center of our state.
The Courthouse building's tall and big,
a building most ornate.

Search for...

Pig   Feather   2 Buckeyes   Pancakes   Snake

Come see the mysterious
Serpent Mound, the
largest effigy in the world.
An effigy is like a carving
of something. And this
mound is in the shape of
a serpent or snake.

It is thought that the head of the serpent, of Serpent Mound, aligns to the
summer solstice, one of the two times when the sun is farthest from the equator.

The state capital resided in Zanesville and Chillicothe for a
short time before moving to Columbus officially in 1816.

River City

Come see the "Genius of Water," at Fountain Square on the corner of Fifth and Vine Streets downtown. The fountain is turned off in the winter and back on at the start of the Cincinnati Reds baseball season!

From Rainforest Gardens to Pretty Pollinators, a scavenger hunt at the Cincinnati Zoo and Botanical Gardens is sure to thrill the green thumb in you! Officially opening its doors in 1875, this Zoo is the 2nd oldest in the country.

If football is your game, catch the Cincinnati Bengals in action at the Paul Brown Stadium. Watch out for 'Who Dey,' the mascot of the team. Think Tiger!

With a fountain full of water, and a city full of fame, Cincinnati and the Bengals most definitely, 'got game!'

Check out the Cincinnati Museum Center. It's a one-stop-museum-going-spot featuring the Cincinnati History Museum, a five-story Omnimax Theater, the Duke Energy's Children's Museum, and the Museum of Natural History and Science.

Search for...

Baseball bat

Cat skeleton

Buckeye

Radio

Old radio tower

In 1869 the first all-professional baseball team was created, the Cincinnati Red Stockings. With their 57-0 season, the Cincinnati Reds introduced America to the game of baseball.

The term "Porkopolis" comes from the days of the pork processing plants in Cincinnati back in the 1820's. The annual "Flying Pig" Marathon is run through the streets of the city in honor of its heritage.

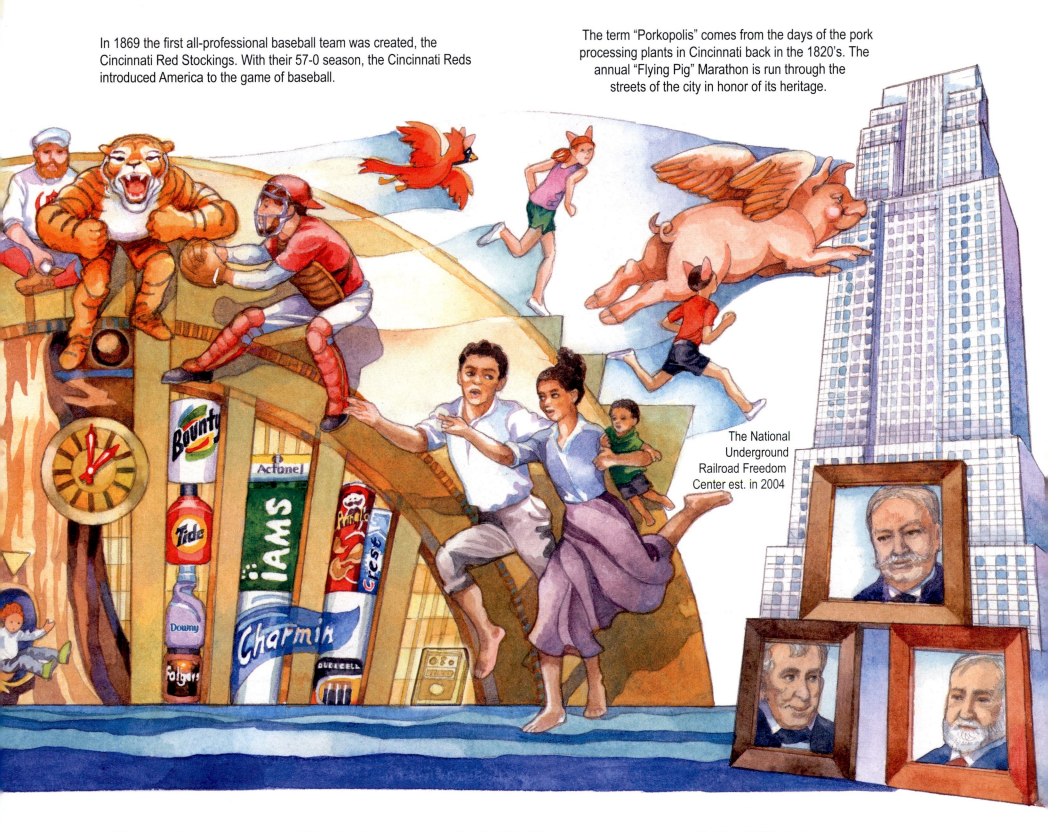

The National Underground Railroad Freedom Center est. in 2004

In 1837, two gentlemen by the names William Procter and James Gamble began their journey of creating products for the home, from soap to candles. Procter & Gamble is headquartered in Cincinnati and makes everything from toothpaste to cat food.

The first 500,000 watt radio station was WLW, broadcast from Cincinnati in the mid-1930's.

What has 8,000 windows, 5,000 doors, and stands 574 feet tall? The Carew Tower, Cincinnati's largest building. Don't forget to elevate yourself up to the 49th floor observation deck for a great view of Cincinnati.

Flying High

You could become an astronomer, a geologist, or an anthropologist, for a day at the Boonshoft Museum of Discovery in Dayton. Rock on!

From bicycles to airplanes,
the Wright Brothers invented flight.
If anyone changed the world,
it was Wilbur and Orville Wright.

The Wright Brothers, Orville and Wilbur, put Dayton on the map, when they lived there and accomplished the very first flight off the coast of North Carolina in 1903. Before they were building airplanes, they were making bicycles. See it all at the Dayton Aviation Heritage National Historical Park.

Search for...

Bicycle

Bug

Buckeye

Goggles

Clay pot

Dayton is known as the Birthplace of Aviation and as the place of many other inventive discoveries. The Inventors Walk in RiverScape MetroPark features inventions including the cash register, the ice cube tray, the Wright Flyer, and many more.

With 1.2 million visitors a year and over 400 aircraft and aerospace vehicles displayed, The National Museum of the United States Air Force at Wright-Patterson Air Force Base is sure to tickle your aeronautic funny bone. Take a stroll on "Air Force One," a VC-137C known as SAM (Special Air Mission) 26000. This is a Boeing 707 and served presidents Kennedy through Clinton. Take a walk on the presidential side!

SunWatch Indian Village of Dayton shares the history of the Native Indian culture and the remnants from the village that were unearthed during archeological digs along the Great Miami River. It is a reconstruction of the 700-800 year old village which was built and occupied by the Fort Ancient Indians who lived there from 1000-1650 A.D. Now that's a long time ago!

Road Trip

We have footballs and farms
and astronauts galore!
Ohio's one great state,
our state that we adore.

Ohio is proud to be the home of 24 astronauts.

Footballs! Footballs! And more footballs! The Wilson Sporting Goods football-making factory of Ada produces over 700,000 footballs each year!

Search for...

Paintbrush

Candle

Buckeye

Mother Goose

Rocket

I-75 is a highway transportation corridor and serves many businesses and industries along its route. This highway is 1786.47 miles long from the tip of Michigan to sunny Miami, Florida. How many of those miles are in Ohio?

John Johnston was a very important man in the early settlement days of Ohio. He served as an Indian agent for the United States government.

Do you love the artwork in children's picture books? The Mazza Museum, at the University of Findlay, has over 3,000 original works of art created by children's book illustrators.

Neil Armstrong was the first man to walk on the moon on July 20th, 1969. He grew up in Wapakoneta. Come to the Neil Armstrong Air and Space Museum just off I-75 and see, up close, his space suit, and a moon rock.

See a Dutch Colonial/Georgian style farmhouse, the two-story spring house and cider house of John Johnston and his wife, from 1829. You will be able to tour the farm, meet costumed interpreters and craft demonstrators, in addition to seeing the preserved ring-shaped mound earthwork from the Adena culture.

Fun's-a-Poppin'

Get your peanuts, get your popcorn,
come play in festival fun!
Come see some great old history,
in magnificent...Marion!

Are you a real history buff? Visit the home of our 29th President, Warren G. Harding and his wife, Florence, and the Harding Memorial, in Marion, Ohio. You will see the 46 columns of white Georgia Marble of the Harding Memorial. While in Marion, you will also want to see a one-room school house, the Linn School.

Warren G. Harding Memorial

Bellefontaine is home to two interesting streets in our country. Court Avenue is the first concrete street built in America in 1801, and McKinley, known as being the shortest, about 20 feet long.

Search for...

United States flag

Popcorn

Buckeye

Shoe

Street signs

Go #29! President Warren G. Harding was born near Marion, Ohio. He moved to Marion after graduating from college, bought a local newspaper, became state senator, lieutenant governor, and later a US senator as well, all before his presidency from 1921-1923.

Can you say Bellefontaine, with a French accent? This is a French word for "Beautiful Spring." The city was originally named "Blue Jacket's Town" by the Shawnee Nation, after their famous war chief, who dominated this area during the 1760's and 1770's until the early 1800's, when American Settlements were established. Ahh! Trés bién.

Stop off at the Palace Theatre to hear the mighty Wurlitzer organ, a real treat!

Don't forget to stop off at Heritage Hall in Marion and visit the Wyandot Popcorn Museum, one of three awesome museums. It features a huge collection of popcorn poppers and peanut roasters. And with the smell, you won't be able to resist some of the free samples. Yum!

The Marion Popcorn festival, a weekend after Labor Day, has lots of entertainment to offer, from a popcorn parade, to a 5k run, a bike tour, beauty pageants, and of course, lots of popcorn!

Between the 'C's

With baskets and bridges shaped like the letter "Y," there's so much to explore, so much for you to spy.

What stands 7 stories tall, has 84 windows, and features two huge basket handles at the top? It is the headquarters of the Longaberger Basket Company.

Search for...

Canoe

Ice cream cone

Buckeye

Mansion

"Y"

Louis Bromfield, a Pulitzer Prize winner and author of 30 books, and conservationist, fulfilled a dream when he purchased a farm. He owned Malabar Farms, where you can now visit and see it, as it was preserved in 1956, the year Louis died. It is now both a working farm and state park. He had many famous friends, including actors Humphrey Bogart and Lauren Bacall, who were married in the thirty-two room mansion in 1945.

Camping, fishing, horseback riding, hiking, canoeing, and swimming at The Mohican State Park is a must. If camping is not your fancy, stay at the nearby hotel that has both indoor and outdoor Olympic sized pools. Splish, splash!

The Longaberger Homestead is located in Frazeysburg. Tour the factory, indulge in some old fashioned ice cream, shop at the Factory store, and of course, see the world's largest apple basket!

The famous "Y-Bridge" in Zanesville, Ohio is the only one of its kind in the world. It crosses over the Licking and Muskingum rivers. This bridge was originally built in 1814 when things cost just pennies. Back then, to cross it, cost 2 ½ cents for each horse and rider.

In the heart

What is a topiary? You can find out at the corner of E. Town and Washington Avenue in Columbus when you see the recreated artwork of famed artist George Seurat, dated back to the 1800's. A bit of culture is good for the soul.

Step back in time to the 1860's at the Ohio Village.

March your way into the heart;
to Columbus, you're our guest.
Toot your horns, beat your drums!
Touchdown! We're the best!

Brutus Buckeye, OSU's mascot, made his first appearance in 1965. One of the team's fight songs, "Hang on Sloopy," is the official rock song of the state.

For all of you garden strollers, stop off at the Franklin Park conservatory. The Palm House features exotic plant displays and the incredible works of Dale Chihuly, the renowned glass artist.

70,000 people take guided tours through the Statehouse each year! That's an average of 192 visitors a day, 365 days a year. You can be a visitor too!

The capitol building, also known as the Ohio Statehouse is huge! It covers nearly two acres of ground and took 32 years to build, from 1839 to 1861. Its initial cost to build was $1.3 million dollars. Can you guess how much it would cost today to build this same building? $100 million.

Search for...

Base drum

Monkey

Buckeye

Pennant flag

Shark

Star

In 1978 Jack Hanna became Director of the Columbus Zoo, and in 1983, he brought fame to the Zoo during his many appearances on major television shows.

The Columbus Zoological Park first opened in 1927 with donated animals. In 1956, the first captive-born gorilla was born at the Columbus Zoo, and his name was Colo. In 1999, when the West Indian Manatees arrived, the Zoo added Aquarium to their name.

Spinning, spinning! Don't look up, or do, but don't get dizzy looking at the Statehouse rotunda! In the top of the dome, a glass skylight is 120 feet up from the floor. The center of the skylight is the 1847 version of the Great Seal of the State of Ohio. The unique floor pattern is made up of nearly 5,000 marble tiles put in place by hand. The center of the floor includes, symbols that pay respect to the 13 original colonies, 3 rings that honor the three territories that expanded our country, and a star with 32 points—the number of states in the union at the time the building was built.

Over 500 football games have been played in the "Horseshoe," home to The Ohio State Buckeyes. In 1936, their band performed "Script Ohio" for the first time. First they form a "triple block O" in the center of the field, and then slowly, while still performing, form the word 'Ohio' in Script form.

First Edition

Library of Congress Cataloging-in-Publication Data on file

Rubini, Julie, Lewis, Anne Margaret and Magnuson, Diana
Hidden Ohio

Summary: *Hidden Ohio* is a fun seek and search book that will share the great state of Ohio and teach new and interesting facts.

ISBN 978-1-934133-47-7
Fiction

10 9 8 7 6 5 4 3 2 1

Printed in Korea

Art Director: Tom Mills
Layout and Design: Sally Bancroft
A Mackinac Island Press, Inc. Publication
Traverse City, Michigan

www.mackinacislandpress.com

Acknowledgements

Nancy Eames, Children's Librarian, Toledo-Lucas County Public Library, Main Library

James E. Mahon 11, Director of Marketing and Communications, Akron/Summit Convention and Visitors Bureau

Christina Thrasher, Kelly Blazosky, Marietta, Washington County Convention and Visitors Bureau

Toni Keller, Marketing and Communications Officer, The Wilds

Kelly Leon, VP of Communications and Community Relations, Fountain Square Management Group

Candace Watson, Director, Convention & Tourist Bureau, Logan County Chamber of Commerce

Lori Kingston, Director of Marketing, Franklin Park Conservatory

Andrew Sawyer, MA, RPA Site Manager, Site Anthropologist, SunWatch Indian Village/Archeological Park

Mark Winchell, Executive Director, Ashtabula County Convention and Visitors Bureau

Media Relations staff at Ohio State University

Martha Otto, Curator of Archaeology, Ohio Historical Society

Staff at Neil Armstrong Museum

Nina Arrowood, Marketing Manager, Great Lakes Science Center

Bev Rose, Director of Marketing and Communications Dayton/Montgomery County Convention and Visitors Bureau

Julie Calvert, Vice President Marketing and Strategic Development, Cincinnati USA Convention and Visitors Bureau

Gregg Dodd, Deputy Director, Communication, Education and Events, Capitol Square Review and Advisory Board

Jeff Glorioso, Director of Sales and Marketing, Columbus Zoo and Aquarium

Jeffrey Helmer, Park Ranger, Perry's Victory and International Peace Memorial

Cheryl Hohne, Mike-Sells Chip Company

Federal Highway Administration, Office of Public Affairs

Patrick Quackenbush, Hocking Hills State Park

Sewah Studios, Inc.

Bibliography

Crawford, Brad. Ohio Compass American Guides, Fodors, 2005

Fradin, Dennis B. With a Little Luck: Surprising Stories of Amazing Discoveries, Dutton Children's Books, 2006

Schonberg, Marcia. All Around Ohio Regions and Resources Heinemann Library, 2003

Weber, Art and Bailey, Bill and DuFresne, Jim Ohio State Park's Guidebook Glovebox Guidebooks of America, 2003

Wright, David K. Moon Handbooks Ohio 2nd edition Avalon Travel Publishing, 2003

Zimmerman, George and Carol Off the Beaten Path Ohio Tenth edition The Globe Pequot Press, 2005

Zurcher, Neil Ohio Road Trips with Neil Zurcher Gray and Company, 2006